AF131406

BOOK ANALYSIS

By Kody Coughlan

Carrie

BY STEPHEN KING

STEPHEN KING

AMERICAN AUTHOR

- **Born in Portland, Maine in 1947.**
- **Notable works:**
  - *The Shining* (1977), novel
  - *IT* (1986), novel
  - *Misery* (1987), novel

Stephen King is an American author best known for his horror novels. Born in Portland, Maine in 1947, King was raised by his mother after the separation of his parents. From there, King spent his childhood between Fort Wayne, Indiana, and Stratford, Connecticut. In 1970, King graduated from the University of Maine with a B.A. in English, and married Tabitha Spruce the year after. It was over the next few years that King's novel writing became recognised. Having published many short stories since 1967, King moved forward and sent his first full-length novel, *Carrie*, to a publication agency by the name of Doubleday & Co., which accepted the novel in 1973. This allowed King to leave his teaching career and write full-time. King continued with his writing career, writing *The Shining* (1977), *The Stand* (1978), and *The Dead Zone* (1979), along with many other novels.

CARRIE

EPISTOLARY HORROR NOVEL

- **Genre:** novel
- **Reference edition:** King, S. (1974) *Carrie*. New York: Doubleday.
- **1st edition:** 1974
- **Themes:** longing for love, revenge, sin, women and femininity, violence, supernatural

Carrie tells the story of Carrietta N. White, a telekinetic school girl in the year of 1979. Carrie is cast as a misfit in high school, and is thus bullied by her peers. She uses her newfound powers to get revenge on those who have tortured, tormented, and mocked her. Newspaper clippings, articles, letters, and excerpts from other books are used in the novel to give most of it an epistolary structure in order to tell the story of how Carrie destroyed the town of Chamberlain, Maine. King himself finds this work rather shocking, with immense power to hurt and horrify its readers.

SUMMARY

TELEKINESIS AND THE SUPERNATURAL

Born with the power of telekinesis, Carrie is capable of manipulating and controlling objects and people with her mind. Despite trying to keep this ability a secret from others, Carrie has had multiple outbursts in front of people, who later choose to ignore what they saw. This apparent blessing turns into a curse as soon as Carrie realises that she cannot control these powers.

Carrie also has the power of telepathy, allowing her to read people's thoughts, yet it is only used once: Rita Desjardin, Carrie's physical education teacher, accidentally reveals her mixed feelings of pity and revulsion through this telepathy, unbeknownst to Desjardin. This ability also works in a reverse manner, allowing others to read Carrie's thoughts instead.

It is unknown whether or not Carrie's dead father also possessed these powers, though it is hinted that he did. Similar to Carrie, her father, Ralph White, may have kept his powers to himself, if he knew about them at all. However, unlike Carrie, he may have never grasped the full strength of his powers, never fully utilising them like his daughter.

TAUNTS, REVENGE, AND ENEMIES BECOMING FRIENDS

Carrie is consistently taunted by her classmates at Ewen High School, particularly by a wealthy, popular girl by the name of Chris Hargensen. In the beginning of the novel, after an incident in which Chris and the other students are interrupted by their teacher, Miss Desjardin, during their taunting of Carrie, Desjardin unsuccessfully attempts to get the students suspended and banned from the school prom. Instead, the girls are merely punished with detention and warned that anyone who skips the detention will receive the original punishment of suspension and exclusion from the prom.

Chris, believing that her harassment of Carrie was justified, ignores the first punishment, refusing to do any detentions, and is therefore suspended. Her attempt at getting her attorney father to force the principal, Henry Grayle, to lift this punishment fails, resulting in Grayle threatening Chris with a lawsuit on Carrie's behalf. This stokes Chris's anger, and she begins to seek revenge.

Another girl who had participated in the earlier teasing of Carrie, Sue Snell, feels guilty and ashamed of what she has done to Carrie, and wishes to make Carrie feel better. She persuades her boyfriend, Tommy, to ask Carrie to prom; Carrie is wary, but accepts nonetheless. Seeing this as the perfect opportunity for revenge, Chris whips up a plan, and quietly has Tommy and Carrie elected Prom King and Queen. Chris's boyfriend, Billy, is forced to kill pigs and collect their blood, and then put buckets full of the blood above the stage at the prom. Once a string is pulled, the blood will spill onto whoever is positioned right underneath – in this case, the Prom King and Queen.

THE PROM AND THE DESTRUCTION OF CHAMBERLAIN

Carrie's mother, a highly religious Christian woman, is infuriated when Carrie makes a red dress for the prom, as she hates the colour red and thinks a school dance, and further, any form of sex, is sinful — even after marriage. She accuses Carrie of witchcraft due to her powers, but Carrie, tired of her mother's lectures on what is sinful, simply longs for a normal life.

At the prom, Carrie finds that Tommy and his friends are quite welcoming, and the night initially goes well for her. The night takes a turn when Tommy and Carrie claim their crowns, and Chris dumps the pigs' blood on the two. Tommy is killed by the impact of one of the buckets hitting his head. This humiliation pushes Carrie over the edge, and after leaving the building, she uses her telekinetic abilities against everyone in the school.

The gym doors slam shut, locking students in, unable to escape. The sprinklers are turned on, and when the singer of the band attempts to address the crowd with a microphone, he is electrocuted. Carrie goes even further, causing the circuit box to explode, which leads to a fire breaking out in the gym, while more students are electrocuted by electrical cables. The fire becomes uncontrollable, and the school is eventually destroyed by a fuel tank explosion.

As she makes her way home, Carrie causes more telekinetic chaos, destroying the rest of the town. Another explosion is caused by the mix of spilled gasoline and a discarded cigarette. As she continues along her destructive path, Carrie uses her telepathy to send out a message to the townspeople, letting them know that everything that has happened has been caused by her.

Carrie returns home, seeking to confront her mother, who thinks the only way to save her daughter, whom she believes to be possessed by Satan, is to kill her. Her mother stabs Carrie in the shoulder, but before she can do much more, Carrie stops her heart with her mind.

Carrie finds the place where she was conceived. Billy and Chris are seen trying to leave, but after an attempt to run Carrie over, Carrie telekinetically takes over the control of Billy's car, and it drives into a wall, killing both Billy and Chris. Sue Snell finds Carrie, and the two speak to one another telepathically. Carrie had been under the impression that Sue and Tommy were involved in the prank, but she now sees that Sue is innocent. With Carrie's dying breaths, she forgives Sue, and cries out for her mother.

THE AFTERMATH AND INVESTIGATIONS

Desjardin survives the fire at the school, amongst a few others. She thinks that the entire chaos could have been avoided if she had reached out more to Carrie. She resigns from her job, along with Grayle. The surviving seniors attend a terrible and bleak graduation ceremony.

Excerpts from reports, including one by Sue Snell are interweaved throughout the book, along with an article written by a surviving student, Norma Watson; interviews with Carrie's mother's family; a woman who was witness to the powerful telekinetic abilities displayed by the three-year-old Carrie, and several others who dealt with the aftermath of the incident. Transcripts from hearings, testimonies, and witnesses are also dispersed throughout. A report declaring that there are no others like Carrie is included, but is contradicted at the end of the novel, where a letter from a woman to her sister talking about her daughter's powers is displayed.

Chamberlain becomes something of a ghost town after being abandoned by its citizens, but it is still a popular tourist attraction.

CHARACTER STUDY

CARRIETTA "CARRIE" WHITE

Carrie grew up a lonely and isolated child. The only child of Margaret and Ralph White, her father left his wife and child, and later died in an accident. Carrie has been constantly abused and neglected by her mother, who is highly religious and mentally ill. This abuse feeds into Carrie's school life, where she is teased and mocked for being different.

While she is seen as an outcast and is at the bottom of the social pyramid, Carrie has a secret that no one knows, not even her mother— she has telekinetic and telepathic powers, but it is hard to say whether they are a curse or a blessing. She becomes aware of these powers when she starts high school, and after an incident where Carrie has her first period, an entire chain reaction of events occurs that leads to the deaths of Carrie and many others.

Carrie's lack of knowledge of menstruation after she gets her first period in the showers at school solidifies her status as an outcast and makes the taunts of the students grow in intensity. Carrie reaches her breaking point after a 'prank' at the school prom, and her hidden powers finally erupt out of her, destroying the school and the entire town.

While Carrie's descent into madness is evident, it is also clear that Carrie was not a villain her entire life. She was not a monster, but rather a young child with a traumatising and fiercely lonely past. She allows her powers to control her rather than her controlling them, and combined with the abuse she has endured, this eventually precipitates her transformation into a murderous monster.

> "[Carrie] is the girl they keep calling a monster. I want you to keep that firmly in mind. The girl who could be satisfied with a hamburger and a dime root beer after her only school dance so her momma wouldn't be worried." (p. 197)

It is the build-up of anger, frustration, loneliness, and hatred that pushes Carrie to the brink. Her efforts to hide her abilities become more difficult as time passes, and the prank at the prom is the final straw. While Carrie's actions are completely unjustifiable, had she had anyone looking out for her, caring for her, or even talking to her in a genuine way, she may have been able to control her powers to a certain extent.

SUSAN "SUE" SNELL

Sue begins the novel as one of Carrie's tormentors. She joins in with Chris during the shower incident, screaming "plug it up!" (p. 4). It is possible that Sue was acting under peer pressure from Chris, due to the guilty conscience she feels afterwards. This is further implied by Miss Desjardin, who says, "you wouldn't expect a trick like that from Sue. She's never seemed the type for this kind of a stunt" (p. 13).

In an attempt to clear her conscience, Sue convinces her boyfriend, Tommy, to take Carrie to the prom instead of her. She is also under the belief that she is pregnant, and therefore stays home on the night of the prom.

It is not until several hours later that the town whistle blows, causing Sue to look out of her window and in the direction of the blazing school. She takes her mother's car to the scene, and watches the school explode just as she arrives. Sue knows that this was the final result of the prank at prom, and that Carrie was acting in revenge and anger.

She finds Carrie, severely injured and dying, next to Billy's destroyed car, where he and Chris lay dead. Carrie allows Sue to explain her part in that night; Sue never truly hated Carrie, and she had no part in the prom prank. She wanted to make Carrie feel accepted by getting Tommy to ask her to prom.

With Carrie's final breaths, she telepathically conveys to Sue just how awful and terrible Carrie's life was, and just how horrible Sue had been to her during the shower incident. Once Carrie dies, Sue identifies her body, and testifies at The White Commission.

Later in life, Sue writes a book which she titles *My Name is Sue Snell*, in which she outlines and discusses the events of the prom from her perspective.

Sue was one of the very few people who were actually nice to Carrie, even if Carrie did not realise it. She had no bubbling hatred for the girl, nor did she wish to see her humiliated and tormented. While Sue partook in previous incidents, it is clear that she was not acting of her own accord.

CHRISTINE "CHRIS" HARGENSEN

Chris is the leader of the group of popular girls at school. She is the daughter of a successful and wealthy lawyer, John Hargensen, and one of Carrie's main tormenters. She leads the jeering during the shower incident. It is this incident that gets her sent to detention, and her lack of attendance at those detentions that gets her banned from prom.

Chris also hatches the prank that is pulled on Carrie — namely, the bucket of pigs' blood that is dropped over Carrie onstage. Chris intended to humiliate and further torture Carrie, in which she was successful, but the final result ends in misery, pain, and death for Chris and many others.

Chris is well known for bullying people she believes to be lesser than her. Anyone who could be deemed unpopular, an outcast, or simply different is tormented by Chris Hargensen, and as a result she has been sent to detention 73 times in four years.

After the prom prank is set in place, Chris and her boyfriend, Billy Nolan, go to a roadhouse to be alone, until they are interrupted by Jackie Talbot, a classmate of theirs. She informs them about the arson taking place at the school, and the fact that the town is burning to the ground as they speak. Chris and Billy attempt to leave town, but not until they try to put an end to Carrie's life.

But Carrie, using her telekinesis, takes control of the car, and Chris and Billy are hurled into the wall of the roadhouse. Another fire breaks out when the car explodes, and the two passengers die at the scene.

RITA DESJARDIN

Rita Desjardin, or Miss Desjardin, is the Physical Education teacher at Ewen High School. It is only her first year at the school and consequently she gets some help from the assistant principal, Mr. Morton.

In the beginning of the novel, she is on the same side as the students when it comes to how they feel about Carrie — disgusted. It is not until she witnesses Carrie being harassed in the locker room after getting her first period that she takes Carrie's side. Desjardin wishes to have the bullies suspended for three days and banned from the prom, but instead, they are given detention, with the original punishment as a back-up. Desjardin believes that the administrators did not go with her punishment because they were all men, and thus did not truly know how terrible the girls had been to Carrie.

At the prom, Desjardin talks to Carrie, telling her all about her own prom night, and later congratulates her on winning the title of Prom Queen. After the incident with the pigs' blood, Desjardin fails in trying to hide her laughter from Carrie, having been impacted by the laughter running through the gym. When she tries to reach Carrie, Carrie refuses to speak to her, using her mind to push her aside.

Desjardin witnesses the entire catastrophe of the prom and the destroyed school, but she is one of the only people who manages to escape and survive.

A couple of weeks after the incident, Desjardin retires from teaching, as she feels guilty about what happened with Carrie and her own behaviour at the prom. Even though she was not the sole reason for Carrie's rampage, Desjardin feels as though she contributed, either directly or indirectly.

ANALYSIS

THE THEME OF LONELINESS AND ISOLATION

Throughout the novel, the theme of loneliness, isolation, and outright exclusion from society plays a critical role in jumpstarting the events that we see. Without feeling any of these, it is quite possible that Carrie would not have allowed her powers to absorb her, controlling and destroying her and Chamberlain; thus, the events of the book would not have taken place. At the beginning, as the girls shower after P.E., joking and talking with each other, Carrie feels like "a frog among swans" (p. 2). She is ignored and made to feel as though she does not belong, which is exactly how her classmates wish her to feel and think.

Carrie's own mother, Margaret, abuses and neglects her, failing to tell her about menstruation, leading to Carrie's humiliation in the showers at the start of the novel. Her mother believes almost everything to be sin, and so keeps her daughter in the dark about a lot of things, including menstruation and sex.

Due to this failure to give Carrie the knowledge she needs growing up, the scene in the showers becomes all the more traumatic.

> "[Carrie] is psychologically a baby among teenagers here, instead of this being a passage from girlhood to womanhood, she's held back by one phase of life, passing from unborn to born, from unknowing innocence to the terrors of the real world, like a newborn baby." (Gorshin, 2017)

This further isolates Carrie from those around her. She is still a child, unaware of the realities of life and growing up. As her classmates taunt and laugh at her, she is crying, terrified and, quite possibly, wishing to escape the horrors of that moment and the life she is living.

Another instance where Carrie is isolated and separated from her peers is the prom. After receiving the title of Prom Queen, the pigs' blood is spilled over Carrie and Tommy. Tommy is killed within minutes from the impact of the bucket, and so Carrie is left alone on the stage.

She is watched and laughed at by everyone in the gym as the pigs' blood drips from her. Carrie is the centre of attention, yet not in a good way. A night that was supposed to be filled with laughter, entertainment, and joy for Carrie turned her into all of that. *She* became the laughing stock, the entertainment for the school, which brought joy to everyone there.

But for Carrie, that singled her out, and drove her to purposely isolate herself, burning down the school and town with her telekinesis. The constant neglect and exclusion Carrie felt growing up resulted in her allowing her hatred and anger to take over. She wanted to inflict the trauma she felt on others, showing them how it felt to be her, and hurting those who hurt her.

INVESTIGATIVE REPORTS, LETTERS, AND TESTIMONIES

The novel's form is epistolary, consisting of articles, books about the incident (*My Name Is Sue Snell*), testimonies, and inquiries into that night. There are no clear answers, nor does anything connect completely. "This breaking up of the narrative flow into fragments, telling the story from different angles, symbolically suggests failed communication, with its starts and stops" (Gorshin, 2017).

These small fragments of an incomplete story can be juxtaposed with the reality of its symbolism — failed communication with Carrie. No one truly communicates with Carrie properly or fully throughout the entire novel, from her mother's failure to discuss puberty with her, to Desjardin's failure to help Carrie out even more.

The story is split up by the articles and reports. There is no direct pattern for when or how these will show up in the story, and so King intertwines them with crucial scenes, such as the prom prank. "We're in [Carrie's] head right up until she gets crowned Queen, and then the pig's blood comes down, and then..." (Hendrix, 2012). The narration switches to other points of view, and excerpts from magazines about the prom night, and transcripts, before actually telling the reader what happens once the climax hits. It keeps the reader on the edge of their seat, wanting to continue reading to see what happens next.

These reports, articles, etc. also give the reader more than one perspective of the night. In addition to King's use of multiple points of view, with the narration switching from Carrie to Chris to Sue, among others, the inclusion of extra snippets gives the story more depth and more complexity. It reads as a report, with the different perspectives not quite matching up, but still coming together to provide a better idea of the full picture.

These different perspectives do not tell the whole truth, nor do they tell a total lie. It may be up to the reader to decide what they believe and how they wish to look at the story.

THE HISTORY BEHIND *CARRIE*

Carrie may have been King's first book to be published, but it was not the first book he had written. Before *Carrie*, King wrote three other novels, none of which were published. *Carrie* began as a short story which King planned to publish in *Cavalier* magazine, but after only three pages, he threw the work into the garbage.

It was not until his wife, Tabitha, pushed him to finish *Carrie* that he decided to actually complete the story. She insisted that she help him with the perspective of the women, and so King persisted, turning the short story into a full-length novel.

Within his book *Dance Macabre* (1981), *Carrie* is stated to be an allegory for feminism: "*Carrie* is largely about how women find their own channels of power..." (King, 1981: 106). While she may be a neglected, miserable teenager, constantly being broken and put down in a world full of men, she is still a woman, and she is finding her strength and her powers for the first time.

The inclusion of telekinesis in the story came from King's personal reading on the topic. "*Carrie* was written after *Rosemary's Baby*, but before *The Exorcist*, which really opened up the field" (Wells, 1980).

It became difficult to write *Carrie*, for King could not relate to any of the problems Carrie had to deal with. He doubted the novel, and lacked in confidence, but it was with the help and support from his wife that he continued nonetheless.

While *Carrie* was being published, King was an English teacher at Hampden Academy, and as he was barely making ends meet, King detached his phone line so as to save more money. He received news of *Carrie* being accepted for publication via telegram in March or April of 1973.

King received an advance of $2500 for the initial publication of *Carrie*, and in May of 1973, the New American Library bought the paperback rights for $400 000. The original hardback sold 13 000 copies, while the paperback sold over one million copies just in its first year.

FURTHER REFLECTION

SOME QUESTIONS TO THINK ABOUT...

- Carrie grows up without any familial love nor any affection from her peers. She longs to feel like she belongs, and longs for affection. Compare this to the *Harry Potter* series by J.K. Rowling (British novelist and screenwriter, 1965-present), in which the titular character feels the same way as Carrie. What similarities and differences can you identify between the two novels?

- Discuss the build-up to Carrie's outburst. What was the initial catalyst for her descent into madness, and how did everything else contribute to it?

- How does each adaptation of *Carrie* differ from each other, and from the original novel? Why do you think the changes in the adaptations were necessary or significant?

- The neglect and abuse that Carrie faced growing up turned her into an incredibly shy girl, yet these events also pushed her over the edge and into the territory of being a monster. Discuss.

- Miss Desjardin is one of the first and only people to show Carrie any kindness, even if her initial reaction to her was disgust. Despite Carrie knowing that Desjardin found her repugnant due to her telepathy, why do you think she spared Desjardin anyway, rather than killing her along with everyone else?

- What do you think became of the woman who wrote the letter at the end of the novel, who brags to her sister about her daughter's display of powers similar to Carrie's?

- Do you agree with King's statement that *Carrie* is an allegory for feminism? Why, or why not?

- Carrie is isolated from her mother, peers, and society in multiple ways. How else can she be seen as isolated and excluded, and further, how does this contribute to the prom incident?

We want to hear from you!
Leave a comment on your online library
and share your favourite books on social media!

FURTHER READING

REFERENCE EDITION

- King, S. (1974) *Carrie.* New York: Doubleday.

REFERENCE STUDIES

- Gorshin, M. (2017) Analysis of 'Carrie'. *Infinite Ocean.* [Online]. [Accessed 18 January 2019]. Available from: <https://mawrgorshin.com/2017/03/04/analysis-of-carrie/>

- Hendrix, G. (2012) The Great Stephen King Reread: *Carrie. tor.com.* [Online]. [Accessed 18 January 2019]. Available from: <https://www.tor.com/2012/10/18/the-great-stephen-king-reread-carrie/>

- King, S. (1981) *Danse Macabre.* United States: Everest House.

- Wells, R. W. (1980) "From Textbook to Checkbook". *Milwaukee Journal.*

ADAPTATIONS

- *Carrie.* (1976) [Film]. Brian De Palma. Dir. United States: United Artists.

- *Carrie.* (2002) [Film]. David Carson. Dir. United States: Metro-Goldwyn-Meyer.

- *Carrie.* (2013) [Film]. Kimberly Peirce. Dir. United States: Sony Pictures Releasing.

MORE FROM BRIGHTSUMMARIES.COM

- Reading guide – *IT* by Stephen King.

www.brightsummaries.com

Ebook EAN: 9782808017442

Paperback EAN: 9782808017459

Legal Deposit: D/2019/12603/39

Cover: © Primento

Digital conception by Primento, the digital partner of publishers.